# Finding
# The
# Strength

# Finding The Strength

Discovering God's strength in tough times.

by

Dave Powers

Harvest Publishing
Newport Beach, California

*Dedicated to the many families who have faced life's disappointments and overcame.*

# Contents

# Introduction

There is no escaping the reality, that life can be a painful experience at times. The suffering brought on by the tough times we face comes in many forms; the sudden loss of a spouse or loved one, a disaster that threatens our security or destroys our home, someone who has taken advantage of us, a friend who betrayed us, or for many, a physical or emotional abuse by someone we trusted. The question is not, how can we keep suffering out of our life? The real question is what will we do with those painful experiences? How we react to the bad things that happen in our life, has everything to do with where our life will go, and what our life will be like in the days ahead.

In these few pages we look at someone well acquainted with loss and suffering. We know him as Job. Through his life and his counsel we will discover that though life brings its fair share of pain and suffering, there is a way out of the wilderness of bitterness and resentment.

Though the journey may be difficult to begin, and even tougher to complete, it is a journey well worth the taking. For at the end there is strength for living life.

# Chapter One

# A Strange Place To Begin

It may seem a strange place to begin our journey, but without a doubt the person who best understands the suffering we face, and the reactions we have, is Jesus Christ. Yes He is the Son of God, and yes He is all knowing and yes He is the greatest teacher who ever walked the face of the earth. But He understood His Disciples, He agonized for His Followers, and on occasion He even wept for a city, for the nation of Israel and for a friend named Lazarus. So when His Disciples faced a tough challenge, His words were not just "church talk". They were heart-felt, well chosen counsel to prepare the people He loved, for something that could have long term effects in their lives.

The Disciples had been with Jesus for better than two years; they had watched Him perform miracles, feed the multitude, teach to the religious and the nonreligious, care for those society had not. In those two years the Disciples had seen a lot. And now it was their turn. They didn't know it, but they were being given their very first assignment to share with others this great news they had seen for themselves. Matthew 10:1 tells us, *"He called his twelve disciples to him and gave them authority to drive out evil spirits and to heal every disease and sickness."* That, in and of itself, should have been a pretty good signal that something was going to happen. Little did the Disciples realize just how much was going to happen. They would be doing, the very things they had seen Jesus doing. That's a mighty tall order to fill.

In the instructions Jesus gives to the Twelve, He gives us an insight to the *life orders* He gives to every person on this planet. Our life orders are simply; "Live a life worth living." But within those few simple words is a host of challenges. The same challenges the Twelve would face. Notice how Jesus prepares the Twelve and us:

The assignment starts off with, *"Go get the sheep, heal the sick, and raise the dead."* All the many days the Disciples had spent with Jesus were not intended to be solely for their personal benefit. There time together was intended to equip them to fulfill their life's mission. When we think about it all the experiences in our life, the good and the bad, have been a building process, equipping us to fulfill our life's mission. No single event was ever intended to be the place where we would stay. And as much as the Disciples may have wanted to just sit around the camp fire with Jesus, that wasn't their purpose. When He called them two years earlier, they had no idea where that invitation would lead them. Jesus knew. He knew there would be a lot of "preparation" needed to equip that small group into world changers. And even this trial run, was only part of the process of preparing them for flying solo.

Life brings a lot of disappointments our way. If we're not careful, our disappointments may take our focus off the reason for our life. They may distract us from soaking up the preparation God has in mind during those times of pain and even grief. The Twelve needed to hear, very clearly, what their mission was, *"Go get the sheep."* And whatever else happened, whatever obstacles they may face, they had their mission to fulfill. But the instructions didn't end there.

Jesus goes on to tell the Twelve He is sending, *"Heal the sick, raise the dead, cleanse the leper....Freely you have received, freely give."* The Twelve needed a reminder, "Your mission is to give away something you didn't earn. Give it away freely." The truth is, sometimes we become stingy with life. We become selective with whom we show our kindness, to whom we say a kind word, or whom we even recognize as being on the planet with us. One expectation Jesus had for this group was to fulfill their mission, and fulfill it with enthusiasm. Even if tough times came their way, Jesus expected their strength to be evident.

Then Jesus begins to prepare His Disciples for some of the challenges they will face as they set out on this mission: *"I am sending you out like sheep among wolves."* Right up front Jesus wanted his Disciples to know, there are people in this world who will take advantage of you, mistreat you, even harm you. This world is a tough place at times. And we know from life experience, He was telling the truth. There are people who intend to cause us pain, who set out to take advantage of us and even cause us physical suffering solely for their own satisfaction. But right on the heels Jesus tells the Twelve, *"Therefore be as shrewd as snakes and as innocent as doves."*

Jesus prepares the Twelve for one of their toughest challenges, people. People can cause a lot of pain in our lives. But His plan for the Twelve is they would be "shrewd as snakes". We may think of that as being sneaky or underhanded, or deceptive. But that's the far from the idea Jesus had in mind. He calls His Disciples to being alert, to pay attention to people and what they say and how they say it. To not open themselves to pain needlessly.

13

We know there are people who have a tough time communicating. They don't always have the right words to express themselves, but their motives are pure. Their heart is in the right place and we can trust them. We also know there are people who know how to "turn a phrase." They know how to say just the right thing to "pull us in", but their motives are impure. They have only a self serving agenda, and perhaps even intend to cause us harm. Jesus wanted His Disciples to be alert. We might even say, "Tough skinned and a tender hearted."

Notice He wants the Twelve to be *'shrewd as snakes and as gentle as doves"*. Regardless what other people may do, how cutting they may be, or how harmful they may want to be, gentleness is the trademark of those who know The Shepherd. And along with that expectation Jesus goes on to tell the Twelve, *"If anyone will not welcome you or listen to your words, shake the dust off your feet when you leave."* When people aren't willing to receive you, when they have made up their minds that their agenda is the only way things can work, shake off the dust and move on.

Shaking off the dust may sound a simple thing to do, but it may be more of a challenge than we planned for. It's the balance between taking the necessary steps to protect ourselves and doing so in a way that reflects whose we are.

# Chapter Two

# Why Does God?

If ever there were a person who had an excuse or even a right to be bitter and resentful we would have to say it is Job of the Old Testament. Without a doubt. His life and the many tragedies of his life are well documented in what many Biblical scholars consider to be the oldest book of the Bible. And there's a reason his story has remained so long.

Job was well-off, perhaps one of the wealthiest men of his times. And his wealth made him a very influential person. We could call him, the Howard Hughes of his day, an influential, wealthy, powerful person. Yet the Bible tells us there was more to this man than his money. In Job 1:8 we are allowed to listen in on a conversation between God and Satan, *"The Lord said to Satan, "Have you considered my servant Job? There is no one on earth like him; he is blameless and upright, a man who fears God and shuns evil."* What a compliment! That God would brag about any of us and hold us up as the glowing example of godly-living. But from that conversation, we also learn that Job did not deserve what was about to happen to him.

Following that conversation, the narrative goes on to tell us life drastically changed for Job. And in that narrative an interesting phrase is used, *"While he was still speaking."* In a series of rapid fire reports Job received a barrage of painful news. The first messenger tells Job that the Sabeans had attacked, stolen all the oxen and donkeys and killed all the servants. The next reported that a lightening storm had killed all the sheep and the servants caring for them. The next reported the Chaldeans had raided and stole all the camels and killed all the servants. The last messenger reported a windstorm had struck the house where Jobs' kids were having a birthday party and had killed all his children and their servants. Each report was followed with, *"While he was still speaking."*

In a single afternoon Job's world collapsed. In a single day he lost everything. His livelihood was taken from him, all his children were taken from him and on top of that, days later he contracted a serious disease that covered his body with painful blisters and sores from head to toe. How quickly his life was turned upside down. One day all was well, the next all hell had been turned loose on him.

We think we have problems! Job certainly had good reason for being bitter. The only thing he had left was a nagging wife. And she gave him all kinds of grief. Then he had his "friends" who came by to cheer him up. With each visit they reminded him, "Job, it's all your fault." Just the kind of friends you need when things are going really bad.

In Job 6:1-3, he shares the weight of his grief with his friends, *"If my troubles and grief were on a scale they would weigh more than the sands of the sea."* Have you ever felt like that? That every single event in your life was one more piece of the weight that was becoming unbearable? In 9:18, Job observes, *"He has filled my life with bitterness."* Was there just cause for Job to be bitter? With all that he had gone through, did he have any grounds to view his life with resentment? Are things that happen to us that cause the same reaction? The answer is yes.

16

Job's situation opens the door to a question that people have wrestled with for years, "Why is there suffering in our life? If God is good, why does He allow bad things to happen?" Several years ago George Gallop did a survey where he asked people across America, "If you could ask God any question and you knew He would give you an answer, what would you ask God?" Far ahead of the second place response, the number one question people wanted to ask God was, "Why is there suffering in this world? Why do you allow it to happen?" Many of us ask that on a regular basis; why do bad things happen to good people, why do we people we trust betray us or why did Mom get sick or why did I loose my job?

As painful as it may be at times, Jesus has always told us the truth about life. As He explained to His Disciples in John 16:33, *"In this world you're going to have trouble."* Although we may never completely understand why God allows evil and suffering in this world, there are some insights to the answer He gives us in the Scriptures. The first being, evil and suffering did not originate with God. In Genesis 1:31 we are told, *"God saw all that He made and it was very good."* What God created was good. So that raises the question, If God did not create evil and suffering, then where did it come from? The answer has to do with God's decision to give us free will.

Now why would God ever give us freedom to make bad choices? We know that part of God's design for His creation is that we would choose to love. To love God and to love one another. And the only way that love can truly be expressed is if we have free will. With free will, we can choose to love or not to love. Because true love involves choosing.

17

My granddaughter received a talking doll for Christmas last year. The kind of doll that has the string you can pull, then the doll repeats whatever it's programmed to repeat. Although the doll can repeat a million times a day, "I love you." Does the doll "love" my granddaughter? No, because it has not chosen to love my granddaughter. It's just doing what it was programmed to do. For any of us to really express love we must be able to choose to do so.

But with the freedom of choice, has come abuse. What was, and is good, we have turned into something harmful by the choices we have made. Our choices have opened the door to evil and suffering. Several years ago a family in the church I pastored lost their son because of a drunk driver. As is the case so many times, the drunk driver had crossed the center line, hit the oncoming car, killing the son and a friend. Meanwhile the drunk driver walked from the accident with only scratches. Several months after the accident I was visiting with the father whose son had been killed and he shared with me a realization he had. He told me, "As much as I wanted to blame God and accuse God of allowing my son to die, I had to finally realize it was through the foolish of a human being, just like me, that our family had suffered. And I thought about what choices I have made that may have caused others to suffer."

There is a lot of suffering brought into this world by our own choices. But we could argue not all suffering is man made. Some suffering is brought on by what appears to be "natural" causes like earthquakes, tornadoes, floods, and wildfires. Natural phenomena that causes pain and suffering. But with a closer examination we discover these too are often the result of the choices we have made. In the

18

Garden of Eden, all creation was responsive to the Creator. But one day Adam and Eve, by their choice, basically said to God, "Thanks for creating us, we can take it from here. We know how to manage our life; we can do better, so we'll take over." And, if we think about it, in part God honored their request. Genesis 3:18 tells us, *"Because of sin, nature was corrupted and thorns and thistles entered into the world."* The New Testament goes on to tell us in Romans 8:22, *"For we know that up to the present time all of creation groans with pain like the pain of childbirth."* It's almost as if nature has been waiting for God, for things to be set right again. But at times nature takes the blame for mankind's poor choices.

Recently we had devastating fires sweep across Southern California. Thousands of acres of land were burnt, hundreds of homes destroyed and seven people died because of the fires. But if we look to the cause of that "natural" disaster we discover that at least two things were the source of the problem: 1.Power lines that had built too close to flammable terrain and 2. An arsonist had set two of the fires, perhaps four. A madman who, for whatever thrill they would experience, ignited dried-parched grass fields and setg in motion a fire storm that caused suffering to hundreds of families.

Our home was in the middle of one of the fires. We, along with hundreds of other families, sat for days waiting for news if our home was still standing. We talked with several friends whose homes did not. As we sat each day, wondering, we began to talk about what the loss would mean. There were all the memories of family gatherings,

19

pictures left behind and even all the work and effort we had put in to make it "our home". But as we talked with friends who had lost their home we heard a different perspective, "Yes we lost our home, but we have our family. Yes, the pictures are gone, but we still have the memories. Yes, it has been a difficult ordeal, but we can start again."

The question has been asked, "If God is all-knowing didn't God know this was going to happen? That people would misuse free will and cause pain and suffering for others in this world. Didn't He know that in advance?" Part of the answer is found in our children. We know that if our kids go to school, or go to the mall, or even step outside our home they will make bad choices. They'll not be paying attention and an accident could happen. They'll try to impress a friend and wind up doing something stupid, like getting a tattoo. We know this, because we did the same things. Not that we did anything "bad" but many times we just didn't do what was right. But even with all the things that could go wrong, do we still let them go to school, or to the mall, or visit with their friends? Yes, because we also know there is the capacity for them to do so many things that are right. They could get a good education, they could laugh and enjoy life with their friends and even at times help their friends make better choices. With all that could go bad, we still choose to let our kids live life, because of the capacity that resides within them to do so much good.

The same thing is true with our Heavenly Father. He knew we could make bad choices, and those choices would bring consequences. But He also knew we could choose to follow Him, we could choose to love others; we could choose to care for others. That the capacity to do what is right resides within us, if we choose to do the right things. For God, the decision was worth it, even though it meant He would eventually have His own Son suffer on a cross.

But since evil and suffering already exist in this world, it raises yet another question: Will there be any good that comes because of evil and suffering in this world? Job begins to unravel that mystery. The suffering in his life is a portal for us to see what the end results could be in our own lives. Someone once said, "Suffering is at least potentially good – an opportunity for good. It's up to our free will to actualize that potential. Not all of us benefit from suffering and learn from it because it's up to us."

If you find yourself understanding, even sympathizing with Job when he says, *"He's filled my life with bitterness"* take the time to finish the journey. Job may have started at a low point, but he was not finished with God, nor God with him.

Job's journey begins on what could best be described as the worse day of his life, and would end on experiencing God in a fresh new way. Against the advice of people who said they loved him. Job sets out to discover the truth about himself and his God. A journey, that anyone who has ever had a tragedy in their life, will need to travel as well.

# Chapter Three

# Root Of The Problem

Our suffering comes in many forms. The first that comes to our mind is usually physical suffering. And it is a painful experience many of us have faced. But there are other forms of suffering we need to investigate. One of the causes of pain in our life is what people say about us. Whether we admit it or not, what people say about us can cause pain in our lives. In Job 12:5, Job is talking to his friends and he says, *"You have no troubles and yet you make fun of me. You hit a man who is about to fall."* Job's assessment of his friends is, "You make fun of me. You laugh at me. You say things about me and that hurts. And you call me your friend." The entire book of Job records a series of hurtful things that Job's friends had to say about him.

Remember when we were in grade school, there was a little saying that went, "Sticks and stones may break my bones, but names will never hurt me." Don't you believe it! Those words do hurt! Labels and pet names hurt and they tend to stay with us. It hurts to be put down or to be made fun of especially in front of other people. We get labels put on us when we're kids that we often carry the rest of our lives. Some of the things we hear when we were children are never forgotten. Something a parent may have said, or a sibling, or a teacher we admired, or even the kids on the playground. Those wounds can hurt for a long time.

Things people say, especially people who are suppose to be our friends, can cause a lot of pain. Solomon was wise enough to include in his Book of Proverbs an insight to this struggle, *"Thoughtless words wound just as deeply as any sword."* His observation is true to life. Words can hurt deeper than even a knife wound and sometimes take a lot longer to heal.

But people can hurt us without ever saying a word. We can all read the nonverbal messages; the body language, the facial expression and even the tone inflections. Have we ever been around someone who, even though they didn't say anything, still made us feel worthless? Listen to what Job says to his friends, *"You think you are better than I am and regard my troubles as proof of my guilt."* Make no mistake, he picked up the signal from his friends, "Job you're worthless."

Besides what we say, there's another way to hurt people, just ignore them. Don't even acknowledge their existence. This is painful to kids and adults alike. And there are people who are pros at this!

One of the basic human needs we all have in common is we want to feel appreciated, we want to feel accepted, and we want to feel approved. Especially by the people who are important in our lives. We will do everything we can to gain the acceptance of the significant people in our lives.

My grandson comes over to our house everyday after school. The first thing he wants to do is to show me what he did in kindergarten that day, even if I have a full schedule. Then my wife reminds me, that my schedule can be set aside for just a few minutes to let our grandson know, he is valued. So I set aside my projects or the book

I'm working on and just listen. And in those few minutes he has my undivided attention and I validate his worth to me, to our family and when he's older to his family. We adults aren't much different, we need the same thing. We're just a little more subtle about it.

The cars we drive, the clothes we wear, even the places we go to buy those items are often crying out, "Notice me! Notice me!" There is a need within all of us to have a life of significance. To know that who we are matters. And someone takes notice of our value.

It hurts when we're trying to please someone, or be noticed by someone, and they reject us. That has happened to many of us when we were growing up. Maybe our best was never good enough, or we couldn't measure up to an older brother or sister. We were just unacceptable. And that pain of rejection remains.

But it's not just what people think or say about us that cases pain, sometimes it what people do to us that causes pain. Again Job is talking to his friends in Job 19:19 when he says, *"Those I loved most have turned against me."* Take note of Job's use of the phrase, "loved most". Those we love the most are those who have the ability to hurt us the most. It's not unusual that one of the causes of our resentment is that the people we're angry with are the people we're trying to love. It's one of the reasons we rarely resent strangers. We don't normally carry bitterness against a stranger. They're just not close enough to hurt us. But it's the people that we are close to that have the greatest impact. The people we're really trying to love who hurt us the most.

Perhaps this is why resentment is most common amongst family members. We find resentment there more than anywhere else. We may be trying to love a parent who was abusive or who neglected us, or we're trying to love a spouse who violated our trust, or even trying to love a family member who misunderstands or manipulates us. That dichotomy between love and hate becomes confusing. And in this confusion the people we really want to love, are often the people we hate, even as we are hoping for something different.

Many of us have grown up with those feelings. We're often trying to decide between, "Do I love them or do I hate them?" The reality is, both are true.

But perhaps the greatest cause of resentment is betrayal; promises that were made and not kept, or a trust that was broken, or even when God should have come through for us, but didn't. It's not uncommon for any of us to feel "betrayed" by God when we loose a loved one, or our livelihood ceases. Whatever its form, betrayal is one of the root causes to the pain and bitterness and even resentment in our lives.

Throughout his conversation with his friends, Job is constantly struggling with the betrayal he must have been feeling. His friends have come to his home because they supposedly care about Job. But more times than not their words reveal a betrayal, "Job it's all your fault. You must have done something wrong for God to do this to you. You need to ask Gods forgiveness." Repentance is easy counsel to give to another.

With all that has happened, it's understandable that Job may even be feeling resentment toward God. After all, wasn't God in charge of his life? Wasn't God the Supreme Being of the universe? Why would God allow such terrible things to happen, to someone so trusting as Job?

It really isn't unusual for any of us to ask these kinds of questions when tough times have come our way. It may even be healthy to inquire into our relationship with God. Having doubts is not a sign of lack of faith. In fact for anyone who is going to have a serious walk with God, these questions will be a part of that journey. And I am convinced that God wants us to bring our questions and our doubts to Him.

When we look at Job's struggle, we find his questions are our own. Many of us face circumstances that seem to defy God's good character. And it's not unusual to look to Heaven with a skeptical eye. But Job also reveals why resentment isn't worth hanging onto.

# Chapter Four

# Letting Go Of The Baggage

As Job's friends counsel him to repent of something he hasn't done, as his wife advises him to just *"curse God and die"*, Job begins to reflect on an alternative. Bitterness and resentment seem like reasonable responses to the injustices in our life. The injustice of when we feel even God has disappointed us. But Job goes through a process of letting go of the baggage that will hinder his journey toward healing. Let's look at the reasons Job gives for letting go of resentment.

First of all, from Job's point of view, resentment is a foolish response to the wrongs in our lives. Note the counsel Job gives in Job 5:2, *"To worry yourself to death with resentment would be a foolish, senseless thing to do."* When we stop and think about it, bitterness is a tremendous waste of our emotional energy. Energy we could be using to bring healing into our lives. Solomon addresses this same issue, look at his counsel in Ecclesiastes 7:9 where he writes, *"It's foolish to harbor a grudge."*

Why is bitterness so foolish? For one reason it doesn't accomplish anything. Harboring a grudge or nursing resentment because of a wrong in our past, will never change the past, nor will it ever correct the problem. To say nothing of the continued damage it will have on our relationships, even sometimes with those who were never a part of the original problem.

We convince ourselves that resentment is making someone else "pay" for what they did, but in reality it doesn't. Most often the person or persons we're trying to hurt with our resentment go on their merry way, totally oblivious to the supposed pain we are causing them. Meanwhile it keeps the pain stirred up in us.

Someone once said that resentment is like setting every calendar in our house, every page of our Day-Timer, the clock on the VCR, anything that shows the time and date, to the day of our pain. So everyday, we are reminded of the past. Everyday is the day of our loss, or the day of our being wronged. Resentment keeps us fixated on the past, never allowing us to heal, never allowing us to enjoy today.

If we could step outside of our lives and watch the movie of our life, we would often see that bitterness and resentment causes us to do some very foolish things. We get hurt, we get wronged and then we get bitter. Then we watch with sad disappointment as the rest of the movie is spent on our trying to get even, or make the perpetrator pay in some way. And we spend a lot of time and energy on something that doesn't really produce the results we were looking for.

Throughout the Bible we find people who have been wronged. Often their response is similar to our own. Take for example, Moses. Called to lead the Israelites out of bondage, things were going pretty good until they got to a place called Meribah, where the people began to complain, accusing Moses of being a terrible leader and in a number of ways make his life miserable. Psalms 106:33 tells us the rest of the story, *"By the waters of Meribah they angered the Lord, and trouble came to Moses because of them; for they rebelled against the Spirit of God, and rash words came from Moses' lips."* Those rash words disqualified Moses from going into the Promised Land. What he had worked so hard for, by his own actions, had become unattainable. God was not going to allow him to enter into the Promised Land; Joshua would be given the assignment. Now before we get too tough on Moses, have we ever done that! Of course! Part of the price tag of resentment is the good things it keeps us from enjoying.

But Job goes on with his counsel in 18:4, *"You are only hurting yourself with your anger!"* Resentment always hurts us more than the person, or persons we are resenting. And again they may be totally unaware that we're holding a grudge. While we're churning on the inside, trying to figure another way to "even the score", they're moving on with life, totally unaware that we're holding onto something they forgot about years ago.

On the evening news we watch with absolute horror as another terrorist straps a bombs to his chest, then steps into a market filled with families and children and pulls the pin. Yes, there's the supposed promise he will get to go to heaven with 70 virgins. But the pain they cause so many others and even the loss of their own life, based upon something that isn't true, is beyond reason.

Resentment is that illogical. It always hurts us more than hurting others. Job was right when he said, *"You are only hurting yourself with your anger."* The price of bitterness and resentment is too high. It's a form of emotional suicide. It prolongs the hurt brought on by the wrong or the abuse.

And keeps us locked to that event for as long as we harbor that resentment.

But Job has one more piece of advice to share, in Job 21:23-25 we read, *"Some men stay healthy till the day they die. They die happy and at ease. Others have no happiness at all. They live and die with bitter hearts."* His observations hold true in real life. We have all seen people who are happy, seemingly well adjusted people and others who spend every moment of their life miserable. And a closer look often reveals that each person has had their own moments of pain, of disappointment and of loss. But their choices made the difference.

Recent medical studies reveal a strong relationship between our emotional health and our physical health. The two have a strong influence on each other. More and more the medical community is realizing that bitterness carries a price tag in our body. It has the ability to cause heart disease, mental disorders, and prolonged body fatigue. Along with that it also drains us of energy, causes backaches, stomach aches and even migraines. Job was right when he says in 5:2, *"Resentment kills."* If we want to be healthy, it's not just what we eat; it's what eats at us! And resentment is like a cancer. It will eat us up from the inside.

If Job is right about his observations of the causes and the price tag of our resentment, perhaps we need to hear him out about how to rid ourselves of resentment. If there's anyone who has earned the right to be heard on this matter, it's Job.

# Chapter Five

# Out Of The Wilderness

The Bible calls us to live a life of peace. In Ephesians 4:31 Paul writes, *"Get rid of all <u>bitterness</u>, rage and <u>anger</u>, brawling and slander, along with every form of malice."* Now that sounds like a pretty big challenge, especially if we have experienced a wrong, or a loss in our life. But Paul doesn't stop there, he goes on to write, *"Be kind and compassionate to one another, forgiving each other, just as in Christ God forgave you."*

How can God expect us to do something like that? Where will we get the ability, or the power to be able to accomplish such a thing? Well Paul gives us one more shot, *"Be imitators of God, therefore, as dearly loved children."* Dealing with our resentment is not a "natural" thing. When everything in us is calling us to get some "pay back", God prompts us to an alternative. The alternative is going to require some supernatural ability. We may not have it in the beginning, but each step will bring more power and more ability to move on to a healthy life.

Have we ever thought about "how" a person can get rid of bitterness and resentment?  Where do we even begin? Well, again Job serves as the person to listen to. We get a first hand look at the journey he traveled out of the wilderness.

The first step of his journey was to be honest and open about our pain. Tell it to God. Listen in on the conversation

Job had with God in Job 7:11, *"I can't be quiet. I am angry and bitter. I have to speak."* (10:1)*"Listen to my bitter complaint. Don't condemn me God!"*

Talk about letting it all out! Job opens the door of his pain and unleashes on God. We may think God doesn't put up with that kind of talk, but it's amazing how big God's shoulders are. He has heard a lot of things through the ages. He has a pretty good idea of what we're feeling before we say it, so say it!

Job goes on, *"Why do you keep me under guard. Do you think I'm a sea monster? I lie down. I try to rest. I look for relief from my pain. But you terrify me with dreams. You send me nightmares. I'd rather be strangled than live in this miserable body. I give up. I'm tired of living. Leave me alone. My life makes no sense. Why is man so important to you? Why do you pay attention to what He does? You inspect him every morning and test him every minute. Are you harmed by my sin, you jailer."* Note what's happening here, Job is letting it all out. Because with all he's been through there has to be a time when he just has to get it out in the open. To unload the weight of all that loss and the pain. And we are no different. It's not out of line, it's not a betrayal of our faith to tell God, "I've had it, and I can't take anymore."

We would expect God to react to Job with, "Who is this guy to question Me?" We would fully expect God to strike Job down for such insubordination. After all, no one has the right to question God, right? But God's response is not wrath, or punishment, or to turn a deaf ear. Instead God's response is, He listens. He is attentive to all that Job has to say and feel.

34

We often mistake God's listening to be God's absence or deafness. That would be a big mistake. Just because God is silent, doesn't mean He isn't listening, or that He doesn't care, or He is not acting on our behalf. Sometimes the best thing God does, is listen. Because if He acted upon ever whim we ever had, there would be a lot more misery in this world. Consider the list of people who have wanted God to act immediately: Moses, "Strike me dead." Elijah, "Strike me dead!" Job, "Just turn your back on me!" King David, "Just turn from me God!" No, we have to admit, God knows when to speak and when to listen. And when we need to unload, He does a pretty fair job of listening.

When we finally come to our senses and cry out to God, "God, I don't like this. This is not right! It hurts!" God's not angry with us. God's not going to be surprised at our response. Who created those emotions? Who gave us the capacity to express our anger and express our feelings? The answer is? (I just wanted to hear you say it.)

When we think about it, God is not at all surprised by our emotional state. In fact He understands more about us, than we understand about ourselves. God gives Job time to vent. His outburst was a catharsis, a cleansing time, a time to let the pressure off. Now we have some alternatives to expressing our pain:

We can keep it in. Bottle up our bitterness, our resentment, and repress those feelings we have, "I'm fine, I'm not bothered by what's happened, the past is the past." And if we shove it down far enough, it will just show up someplace else. Someone once said, "When we swallow our anger, our stomach keeps score." And that's the truth. Or,

35

We can dish it out. Take it out on people who aren't even part of the problem. They have no clue why we are so demanding, or short, or so rude with them. And we wonder why our relationships can't seem to stay together. Why friends don't return calls? Why family keeps at a distance? Everyone else in our life is paying the price for our pain. Or

We can send it up. Take it to God as Job did. Just as Moses, Elijah and David did. They expressed it to God. The Bible is has a long list of *One Another* instructions. Things like; pray for one another, confess your sins to one another, forgive one another, care for one another. God has built within His game-plan called the church a system designed to enable us to take our resentment and give them to God.

Now it's true that over the past few years, the people in His church have let down on this job. Often taking advantage of the vulnerability of the very ones God intended them to care for. So we must be alert, take our time finding the right people we can trust, even in the church, with our openness and our pain. But even with the mistakes people in the church have made, the Bible tells us to, *"Confess your faults one to another whereby you may be healed."* Revealing our feelings is the beginning of healing. And Job may not have known the clinical name for what he was doing, but he was on his way to healing. The problem is if we hold it in, if we keep it a secret, that secret has power over us. But when we tell God, or tell a friend, we take the power out of the secret.

We all need, a friend, at least one good friend who is willing to accept us, unconditionally, even when we're bouncing off the walls. Someone we can just unload on and who will stay with us till we're ready for healing.

Note what Job has to say in 6:14, *"A despairing man should have the devotion of his friends even though he forsakes the fear of the Almighty."* We all need Christian friends who will be our friend even when we say, "I don't trust God right now." And they are willing to stay with us and nurse us back to faith. The Bible says, *"There is a friend who stays closer than a brother."* Those are friends worth having, wouldn't you agree?

Before we move on, if you've had a friend like that, why not take a quick second to give them a call, or drop them a note? If they've been there for you, let them know it is appreciated, and you are in a healing process (maybe just the beginning) because of their help.

I've been told a number of times, "Dave, I had something happen to me. It's over and done but it still haunts me. How can I put that behind me? How can I close the door to my past?" The first place to start is letting it out. Someone once said, "There is no closure without disclosure." As long as we keep it a secret it's going to haunt us. Once we take that first step we are ready for the second, which is:

We need to release our offender. As difficult as this sounds, we will never get past the pain until we forgive. Notice what Job does, in 42:10, *"After Job prayed for his three friends, the Lord made him prosperous again and gave him twice as much as he had before."* Now let's take a good look at this. When did Job's pain end? When he got revenge? After he made them pay? No way. Job gets relief from his

37

misery after he forgives his friends. The account tells us that he "prayed for them." He not only forgave for himself, he asked God to bless them. Even with the pain they had caused him, Job knew he couldn't move on until he forgave. It's kind of tough to resent someone, and ask God to bless them at the same time.

Job was not the last to do this. Remember the story of Joseph and the coat of many colors? As the story goes, Joseph was favored by his father and the other eleven brothers took exception to that. They became so bitter they eventually sold Joseph into slavery to some slave traders heading for Egypt. And through a series of events, most of them not good, Joseph eventually ends up in prison for a crime he did not commit.

This is a part of Joseph's story we overlook. While he sat in that dungeon for a crime he did not commit, what went through his mind? What was the "best" he could hope for? Well, being released of course. His hope was that the day would come a judge would review his case, and he would be set free. But sitting in that prison, the last thought he would have had was, "One day I'll be as powerful as Pharaoh." We often see our prisons from that same point of view. Nothing will ever happen; we've been overlooked by God. But that was not Joseph's story and it is not ours.

Joseph is released from prison, and then goes on to become second in command to Pharaoh. Who puts him in charge of taking care of the food supplies because a famine was on its way. And sure enough when the famine hits, who shows up asking Joseph for food for their family? The eleven brothers.

Through a series of events, the day finally comes when the brothers discover that the one calling the shots in Egypt, the one who decides whether they live or die, is their long lost brother Joseph. Besides being afraid for their lives, the brothers have nothing left to do but receive whatever punishment Joseph decides to dish out. And as they waited for his judgment, which they very much deserved, Joseph decrees, *"What you meant for harm, God meant for good."* Those few words are loaded with meaning. They reveal a man who looks at his life as more than just a series of random events.

How can we know when we've really released that person who has brought so much pain into our life? When we have a moment of evening the score, and we decide the score has already settled. When we could do harm in return for what they have done and we do good. When we not only wish them well, but put our effort behind well being done on their behalf. Then we know we have released them.

Jesus had this to say in Luke 6:27 *"But I tell you who hear me, Love your enemies. Do good to those who hate you. Bless those who curse you. Pray for those who mistreat you."* He says do the exact opposite of our human nature. Instead of paying back, ask God to bless. Instead of snubbing them whenever possible, pray for their well being. Why would God ask us to do something like this? So we can see for ourselves who is in control of our life.

When we return a hurt for a hurt, an eye for an eye, that's simply retaliation. And though we feel "pay back" satisfies, in reality it does not and it reveals we are still controlled

39

by our past. We are being controlled by the pain of our past. God wants to be in control of our life. And He wants us to see His control in action for ourselves.

We often view love as a passive sort of thing. It's not just good feelings or thinking good thoughts toward others. But God's love, the kind He wants us to demonstrate in our own life, is a very active thing. Look at how active God's love has been toward us. Romans 5:8 tells us, *"But God demonstrates his own love for us in this: While we were still sinners, Christ died for us."* While we were still stubborn and defiant, God loved us.

Job's journey out of the wilderness of resentment began by letting it all out with God. But he was wise enough to know that was not the end, it was only the beginning. And if he was ever going to move on with his life, he had to do for others what he was hoping God would do with him, forgive.

But that's not the end of the journey. As a result of Job's actions, a series of events begin to unfold. Job see's the results of a hard traveled journey and the evidence the trip was truly worth taking.

# Chapter Six

# Reaping & Sowing

It may be easy to move to the end of Job's story, the part where all ends well. In Job 42 we read, *"The Lord blessed the latter part of Job's life more than the first. He had 14,000 sheep, 6,000 camels, a 1,000 yoke of oxen and 1,000 donkeys.* It's good to see when a person who has experienced a loss, enjoys restitution. But Job's list continues.

*"And he also had seven sons and three daughters. Nowhere in all the land were there found women as beautiful as Job's daughters, and their father granted them an inheritance along with their brothers. After this, Job lived a hundred and forty years; he saw his children and their children to the fourth generation. And so he died, old and full of years."* Now that's the part of the story we like. We all love to see a happy ending. But there was a long road for Job from chapter one to the end of chapter forty-two. And that road included coming to terms with the wrong that had happened in his life.

It may cross our mind, "I'd like to do what Job did. To be able to move on and leave my bitterness behind, But what happened to me wasn't fair. I didn't deserve what happened to me." And Job's reply would be? "Who said life was going to be fair."

When Job's wife gave him the counsel to just "curse God and die". Job's reply was, *"Shall we accept good from God, and not trouble?"* Job understood that God never promised life was going to be an easy ride. We fouled that up in the Garden of Eden when we told God we could do it on our own.

Long before it was written Job had a grasp of what needed to happen in our lives. Romans12:17 says, *"Do not repay anyone evil for evil. If it is possible, as far as it depends on you live at peace with everyone."* Does God know there are some people we just can't get along with on this planet? Most certainly. Does He also know there are people who have made up their minds they intend to cause us harm? Without a doubt. Job began putting this principle in motion even before it was in print. Look at what Job chooses to do in 11:13, *"Put your heart right, reach out to God then face the world again, firm and courageous. Then all your troubles will fade from your memory, like floods that are past and remembered no more."*

It really does become a matter of what we focus on. The Bible goes on to say, *"Do not take revenge, my friends, but leave room for God's wrath. For it is written, 'It is mine to avenge. I will repay,' says the Lord. On the contrary, if your enemy is hungry, feed him. And if he's thirsty, give him to drink."* What God is calling us to do is, "Get your attention off of how to make him pay, and focus on how to meet his needs."

Several years ago I worked with a man who was a tyrant. He was demanding and abusive of anyone he had authority over. No one wanted to work for him or with him. And I have to admit, I was one of those people. The longer I tried to "live up" to his standards, the more abusive he became.

It took me quite a while to see how this Bible teaching could apply to my situation. I thought a lot about what I was going to do; maybe find another job, or tell him off, or just live with it. I began to think, "What makes this man like this?" So I went, what I like to call, fishing. Fishing to better understand him.

Whenever I could, I would ask him about his life, his past, his family, where he was from and so forth. Over time I discovered a man who had an absent father, an abusive mother, who blamed him for his father leaving, and a long history of just never measuring up in the eyes of the significant people in his life. Well it took time, a lot of time to build a bridge. To support his role as leader, to find the things I could honestly compliment him about.

The day came when the unthinkable happened. He called me into his office to ask my advice about something. It wasn't a big deal, but it was an opening. And I used that as the opportunity to gently show him some of the pain he was causing in other peoples lives. We reached a point where I could go to him privately and talk about a situation where he had been a little too rough on someone. I'd like to say that his life was changed by our conversations, but that's not the case. But there were changes he attempted to make but without the power in his life to help him, those changes were only temporary.

Have we ever heard someone say, "I'll never be like my dad or mom! Or never like that person!" What are we focusing on? The very thing we don't want to be. The fact is, unless we change our focus, that's exactly what we will become. We are drawn to what we are focused on. If it's getting even, we are drawn to getting even. If our focus is finding healing, we'll find it for ourselves and for others.

Job knew there was a process he needed to go through to get refocused. In his advice to his friends in 11:13, he says, *"Put your heart right."* That would be the forgiveness part. It's the best place to begin. Now you may be saying to yourself, "There's no way I can do that. I can't forgive!" That's all the more reason why we need Christ in our life. He will give us the power to do that.

Then Job goes on to say, *"Reach out to God."* Yes, it may have been a long time since we really talked with Him, but He's still listening. Open our heart to Him and ask Him to heal the wounds. And then do that again tomorrow, and the next day and the next day, until we can say, "He is my Healer." And then we'll be ready for his last piece of counsel, *"Face the world again firm and courageous."*

For many of us, when we're hurt, we build a wall around ourselves. It is our way of saying, "I'll never get hurt again!" So we withdraw from life. Job counsel is, "Don't do it!" In fact after, *"Putting our heart right, then reaching out to God"* the next logical step is to get back in the race. Start sharing our life with someone else. Perhaps even someone who is where we have been.

There's a great ending to Job's life in 42:12, *"Then the Lord blessed the last part of Job's life even more than he had blessed the first."* Job went through a lot of pain, a lot of disappointment, but in spite of all that, God blessed the last part even more than He had the first. Deep down inside that is something most of us hope for. We hope that our loss, or our pain, or our suffering will not be wasted. And the reality is, it is not. God never dangles us over the pit of misery just to watch us squirm. That goes contrary to His character. At the core of His being, who God really is, is love. He cannot do anything other than love us.

Job models for us that even though our loss may be great, that our pain is more than we can bear at times, God is not distant. Even when we raise our voice in protest, He has BIG shoulders and a loving heart.

What will the second part of your life be like? Yes, the sting of the past hurts even in the present. But we know the steps God wants us to take. What will your next step be?

The lessons we learn from Job's life are these; it doesn't matter how we've been hurt, or how long we've been hurt, or how deeply we've been hurt, God can make the next part of our life, the best of our life. If we're willing to follow His lead.

We need to ask ourselves: What are the painful memories we're holding on to? Did someone say or do something, maybe even years ago but we've never gotten past it? Perhaps we were abused, or neglected, or a trust was betrayed. When our memory is triggered, it hurts just like it was yesterday! Resentment and bitterness does some strange things to us. Maybe we need to make peace with a parent, a sibling or close friend? We love them, and yet it's frustrating, because we hate them at the same time. That was confusing when we were kids; it's still frustrating as adults.

God is ready to go to work in our life. It begins with something as simple as a prayer. The events of our past don't have to control our tomorrow. We can discover just as Job, and Joseph, and Elijah and millions of people since have discovered, that life *after* can be fulfilling again. If anyone could tell us the benefits of taking this journey, it would be Job. His counsel, *"Put your heart right, reach out to God then face the world again, firm and courageous. Then all your troubles will fade from your memory, like floods that are past and remembered no more.",* is counsel we can depend on. And our journey can be the same as Job's and we can begin even today.

# Chapter Seven

# The End Result

We can all agree suffering is not good. But Job, Joseph, Jesus and many others have shown God can use suffering to accomplish good. If we take the time to look, we discover there are several different ways God does this. The first being that our pain and suffering can draw us and others to Christ. The truth is, for most of us, we tend to learn the hard way. C. S. Lewis once said, "God whispers to us in our pleasure. But He shouts to us in our pain. Pain is God's megaphone to rouse a deaf world."

Many of us know that to be true in your own experience. If we're going through times when everything is going great, the sun is shining, the money is rolling in, the job's secure, we're much less likely to turn to God because we don't need God. But when there is a loss, when there is pain, when suffering comes into our life, what's the first thing we do? We cry out, "God, help me! I need You! I want You! Lead my life! Help me in this situation."

Paul understood first hand our struggle, in II Corinthians 7:10 he writes, *"For God sometimes uses sorrow in our lives to help us turn away from sin and seek eternal life."* And then he writes something that may be difficult for us to agree with, *"We should never regret His sending it."*

Talk about going to extremes! We should never regret that God allows pain or suffering to come into our lives. Why? Because it leads us to reexamine, to reassess and even to repent at times. And Paul was sharp enough to know, that if pain causes us to seek and find God, it is a journey worth taking. Job experienced that firsthand. As did Joseph, and Elijah, and Peter, and Paul, and anyone else who has ever lived on this planet and faced disappointment or loss or suffering. But that encounter with God leads to another good God accomplishes.

God can use our suffering to change our character. Romans 5:3 tells us, *"We also rejoice in our suffering because we know that suffering produces perseverance, perseverance character, and character hope."* Perhaps you've heard the old saying, "No pain, no gain." Nothing gets us to look at the shallowness of our character faster than suffering.

Several years ago I was a runner. I thoroughly enjoyed running and had even raced in a couple of 10 K's. But with all the miles I put into practice between races, I discovered my times weren't improving. One day I was talking with a friend about my frustration and he volunteered to go running with me. Because he had found that two runners training together could be more effective. So early one morning we met for a "light run". It didn't take me very long to discover I had a problem, my friend was gooood. He set such a pace that it took everything in me just to keep up for the first mile. He would slow down at times, but then pick up the pace just as quickly. But after a few runs, I began to keep up. And an amazing thing happened, my times in my next race where greatly improved.

Did I like that burning sensation in my legs and lungs? Did I stop my friend every time we ran to thank him for making me feel like I was going to die? And the answer is, no? But did I like the results of the effort, absolutely. The truth about most of us is that without pain, without suffering, our character would not change one bit. And God certainly understands that about us. Character development is an arduous task.

One of the greatest insights to this process of character development is found in an often overlooked passage of scripture found in Hebrews 5:8 which read, *"Even though He was God's Son He learned to be obedient because of His sufferings."* We understand that there was nothing wrong in Jesus' character. So God wasn't trying to change something in Jesus, He was strengthening something that was already in His Son's character. And there's much in our character that needs to be strengthened.

So God can use our suffering to develop our character but he also uses suffering to discipline us. Now we most often think of discipline as punishment. Something our parents did when we misbehaved or were disobedient. But discipline goes much deeper than that. The ultimate objective of discipline is trust. Hebrew 12:19-11 tells us, *"Our fathers disciplined us for a little while as they thought best. But God disciplines us for our own good that we may share in His holiness. No discipline seems pleasant at the time, but painful. Later on, however, it produces a harvest of righteousness and peace for those who have been trained by it."*

The key phrase there is, *"for our own good"*. God has a bigger view of our life than we do. We're limited by the here and now, by our finite minds and understanding. God has the bigger picture of how He can actually use suffering to actually accomplish something in our lives, how to use discipline that will actually be beneficial for us.

Several years ago our family dog got into the garage and started nosing around where he shouldn't and his nose got him in trouble. He got a fish hook caught in his nose. Now to take out a fish hook, you have to cut the barb end of the hook off then push it back through. As painful as that sounds, and it is, it is the best way to remove a fish hook. Now try as I may to hold the dog still so I could "help him", all he could tell was I was pushing on this metal thing and it was causing more pain than if I just left it alone. What was my objective, to hurt the poor dog or help the poor dog? But from his perspective all he could see was the pain I was causing him.

That's a great analogy for us and God. Many times, most of the time, we don't understand why God allows something to happen, why He allows it to remain and why the process of fixing the problem is as painful as it is. Often we don't see because of our limited perspective. So we wind up blaming Him and even cursing Him for what has happened to us. Why? Because we can't see the bigger picture, the good God is bringing about because of our suffering.

But let's go back to our family puppy for a minute. Eventually we did get the fish hook out, his wound healed and he learned to stay out of the garage. Was there anything positive about his ordeal? As much as a dog can

50

learn, he learned how much every person in our family cared for him. My youngest son would sit next to him everyday for a week just to pet him and care for him. But that dims in comparison to the good God accomplishes. Romans 8:28 tells us, *"And we know that in all things God works for the good of those who love Him, who have been called according to His purpose."* Our Heavenly Father is saying He can take the bad circumstances that overwhelm us and He can cause good to come about if we follow His lead and commit ourselves to His purposes. Note, it's in all things. God works. The good and the bad of life.

There's one last thing we need to consider about suffering, there will be a day when there will be no more suffering. Perhaps you've heard someone say, "If God has the power to stop the suffering in this world, why doesn't He do it?" And the short answer is, just because He hasn't, doesn't mean He can't, nor does it mean that He's not going to sometime in the future. God promises there is a day coming when evil will be judged and suffering will cease.

We watch on the evening news another story of a senseless murder. No suspects, no one brought to justice and we may think, "There's another time when the injustice of this world has gone unchecked. Another time someone got away with murder." But the story of the life of the people on this little blue dot is not finished. God has said He will judge that person and every person who has done evil or caused pain and they will be held accountable for the wrongs they have committed. No one is getting away with murder.

And we may ask, "Why doesn't God come back now?" The short answer is, because He loves us. That may seem strange but 2 Peter 9:3 tells us, *"The Lord is not slow in keeping His promise as some understand slowness. He is patient with you not wanting anyone to perish, but everyone to come to repentance."* What's God saying? In essence He is saying, "I'm going to hold back the closing curtain of history, I'm holding off on judging the world, because of you. I want every person in the world to have every opportunity possible to be a part of my family and be called a child of God." Because ultimately each one of us choose whether to run to God or from God when we have pain or suffering in our life.

We've all seen people who have gone through virtually identical sets of suffering to someone else, only to watch a vast difference in their response. One person becomes bitter, angry, and runs from God. They become sullen and distant to others. And yet someone else having gone through a very similar experience, we watch as their heart is softened by the experience. They become more loving toward God and toward other people. They run to God. And their relationship deepens because of it. Every pain, every hurt, every loss becomes our moment of choice. Job knew he had a choice to make. He could remain bitter and distant from God, but there's no life in that decision.

Job knew that it's difficult, if not impossible to love a God who is distant, uncaring, not interested, and just watching our suffering from a distance. Even before Jesus ever said the words, Job was accepting the invitation, *"Come unto me you who are weary and heavy laden, and I will give you rest."* The end of our journey with suffering leads us to The One who can say better than anyone, "I know what you're going through." He knows what it feels like to lose someone we love. He is well aware of the pain of friends mistreating us, or people who should be trusted, betraying that trust. The bottom line to our suffering is Jesus.

I have no idea what pain you have gone through or may be going through right now. You may find yourself saying as Job did, *"If my troubles and grief were on a scale they would weigh more than the sands of the sea."* But there is One who watches over us. There is a Shepherd, a Shepherd who cares you each of us. And in our darkest times we can find that the Psalmist was right when he was led to write, *"The Lord is my shepherd, I shall not want."*

Isaiah the prophet told us that the Messiah would be a *"man familiar with sorrows."* And certainly Jesus was familiar with sorrow. But not only is He familiar with our suffering, when we put our trust in Him, He lives inside of us and empowers us to face our darkest day. The Psalmist in 34:18 tells us, *"The Lord is close to the brokenhearted and saves those who are crushed in spirit."* When we become crushed by the weight of everything this ole world has to throw at us, there is the source of peace that passes understanding.

What often happens when we're facing a tragedy is we stop living. We don't laugh anymore, we don't enjoy friends, and we allow life to pass us by. In essence we become a different person. But let's go back to where we started in this treatise. When Jesus sent the Twelve out on their life mission He told them right up front, they were *"sheep amongst the wolves"* and they were to be as *"shrewd as snakes and as gentle as doves"*. He wanted them to be ready when the tough times would come. That even in the tough times they would be the same person. And we know that from history that most of the Twelve suffered a martyr's death because of their faith. But that was just one chapter in their life.

There's an interesting insight to what God allows to happen in our life. It comes from I Corinthians 10:13 which reads, *"No temptation has seized you except what is common to man. And God is faithful; he will not let you be tempted beyond what you can bear. But when you are tempted, he will also provide a way out so that you can stand up under it."* God goes on record to let us know that the events in our life are under His constant watch. And yes they are painful at times. As painful as they are to others who have experienced the same things we are going through.

There is a key found in this passage. It is the key that unlocks our ability to cope when facing tragedy or loss. It's found in the few words that read, *"He will also provide a way out so that you can stand up under it."* Job was not given the option of avoiding his suffering. Joseph was not given a choice whether he wanted to go prison for two years. Jesus was not given an alternative to the things He suffered. The events of our lives are not random acts of coincidence. They are the intricate details of our life that make us who we are. And when we are facing our darkest days we find out who we are by what our focus is on. If all we see is our suffering, if all we see is the wrong in our life, then it should be of no surprise to us that we are on our own. There's no need to expect any help from Heaven. But if in the midst of our dark times, even with the grief or pain we are facing, our heart cries out to God and we look with anticipation to the way out He has prepared we will know for ourselves that we are relying on God. And God always keeps His word. Now we can look with confidence to *"the way out so we can stand up under"* whatever circumstances have come to us in this chapter of our life. It is the tough times in our life that allow us to discover who we really are. To examine the basis for our joy and to reexamine the reason for our life. Even the tough times are only a chapter in our life story. And through our tough times we may even discover what the next chapter in our life will be.

What will be the next chapter in your life?